On the Wagon

All about alcohol

Real life experiences of alcohol dependency

and ways to deal with the addiction

Janey Jackson

On the Wagon

Text copyright © 2014 Janey Jackson

All Rights Reserved

On the Wagon

To my children, Tommy, Justin and Joe

On the Wagon

TABLE OF CONTENTS

Preface		5
Introduction		6
Chapter 1	Definitions, Etymology, History of Alcohol	9
Chapter 2	Known causes of alcohol dependence and early warning signs	15
Chapter 3	Physical and psychological effects of alcohol abuse and other consequences	20
Chapter 4	What life might be like to live with someone with alcohol dependency	26
Chapter 5	Ways to overcome alcohol dependency and help for those living with an addict	32
References		46

On the Wagon

Preface

Having been in a relationship for over two decades with someone who had a dependency on alcohol, I now have a much clearer and thorough understanding of the worry, distress and frustration borne by those who live with an addict as well as the detrimental impact the excessive drinker is having on him or herself. Part of this awareness comes from the emotional stress of suffering the constantly changing moods, the peaks and troughs of the drinker's volatile frame of mind but also having to take the brunt of much of the blame for their situation and feelings of desperation. This is far from an easy burden.

In the past, concealing the alcoholic's secretive and dysfunctional behaviour, went hand-in-hand with the marriage vow, *'til death do us part'* and the adage, *'sticking together through thick and thin'*. A good relationship cannot however survive the rigours of such a tumultuous existence. If there are children involved and the drinking has got to such a level that the anti-social behaviour threatens the safety of all the family, this is not an environment conducive to a happy and healthy existence. The experience has provided me with an alternative way of thinking, a way which will not only benefit those living with an alcoholic but ultimately those who are drinking excessively too.

In this relatively short book entitled *'On the Wagon'*, I hope to have succeeded in showing some understanding and compassion to those who have chosen to indulge in a recurrent and harmful pursuit and to try and make them aware of the potentially damaging effects they are having on themselves, both physically and psychologically, and also of the often irreconcilable impact their drinking can have on those who live with or care for that person.

The sad realization suddenly hits you that a considerable part of your life has been irretrievably lost owing to inertia and merely waiting for the problem to rectify itself. Much additional time is spent dwelling on how things could have turned out, had the circumstances been slightly different or the right sort of advice or help been given at the appropriate time. I have written this book therefore, to offer as much support and retrospective advice possible to those who wish to help themselves or a loved one turn their lives around and quit drinking and to identify some of the early warning signs of alcohol dependency in order that the situation can be rectified before there are irreversible consequences. Most important was to offer as much support and advice possible to those living with an alcoholic and provide useful strategies to put an end to this destructor of health and relationships before *it* puts an end to us.

On the Wagon

Introduction

Unless you are a complete teetotaler, no one can deny that there is nothing quite like a cold refreshing beer on a hot sunny afternoon, a chilled bottle of wine shared with friends whilst out for a meal or a few shots before heading off to shake one's booty at the nightclub. There is nothing particularly wrong in fact with a 'Friday night out with the lads', a little bit of Dutch Courage before a wedding, getting slightly tipsy when enjoying the company of an old friend or a few bevvies at the Sunday barbeque. What *is* wrong however, is when we start depending on alcohol all the while for our relaxation, our courage, our happiness, our denial of problems and basically to cope with each and every situation which life throws our way. It is wrong if to drink alcohol is the first thing we think of as we wake up in the morning or the first thing we turn to when we arrive home from work. If it makes us shirk our duties, alter our behaviour towards our loved ones, affects our otherwise sound judgement or entices us to do things which endanger ourselves or others, or for which we need total sobriety, it is wrong.

Fortunately, despite the fact that alcohol is abused by a minority of drinkers, it still proves to be beneficial to the majority. Used as beverages throughout history as thirst quenchers, alcohol is also consumed to facilitate social gatherings, aid relaxation, to accompany and complement the pleasure of food and can, in some cases, help as a medicinal remedy.

Knowing where to draw our limitations has always however posed a dilemma and we shall consider how much harder it becomes when we have poor self-restraint or a gluttonous nature, when stressors in our life get too much to handle or when we mix with the wrong type of company The following chapter will demonstrate how hard it is to define an alcoholic, how difficult it is to decide what quantity, what alcohol content, or with what frequency we can drink alcoholic beverages before we are officially classified as dependent upon alcohol. Some may think they are alcoholic when they are not but worse still we may not realise, (or be willing to acknowledge) the fact that we have a problem when we most clearly do.

Some of us can quite happily sip at one drink all night and be condemned as a 'lightweight' or a 'party pooper'. Others of us can steadily 'go for the gallon' or succeed in drinking our friends 'under the table'. For most people however, knowing our personal limits and preferences is easy. We stop when we feel we might have 'had enough' and be capable of declining the ever tempting offer of 'one for the road'. If we don't, we are still able to anticipate that there might be dreadful consequences for our

On the Wagon

actions. The negative consequences of too much alcohol are too numerous to mention here but some of the obvious ones are listed here with their possible outcomes:

Alcohol makes you forget about time. Therefore at best you might upset 'the other half' for staying out too late and arrive home loudly, slurring your words incoherently and clumsily staggering about. Nothing too bad here you think.

You might forget to pick the kids up from an after school activity. A complete stranger might offer them a lift home instead. A little bit more disconcerting?

You stay out drinking on a weekday. You won't feel like getting up early to go to work the next day, so slam your hand down on the alarm and 'throw a sickie' (one of the most frequent reasons for workplace absence). A possible risk to your job? Employers keep track of dubious absences.

If you do however make it in to work, your excessive drinking the night before makes you feel queasy while at work. You may suffer from blurred vision and endanger yourself whilst operating machinery. You could fall asleep somewhere and run the risk of getting caught. Now your safety *and* job are being compromised.

After-effects of the alcohol may make your hands shaky, you can't concentrate on the computer screen, you repeatedly abandon your work station to make yourself a strong coffee or else to throw up and you will get irritable with your colleagues and belligerent with your boss. This is at least worthy of a reprimand from your bosses, maybe even a verbal warning.

You drink yourself into a stupor and pass out unconscious in the chair. OK, wise choice to drink at home, or is it? Do you want your children seeing you in this disgusting state? You are their role model and shape their behaviour later in life. Are you going to be kind and affectionate to your partner when you come back round? Was this what you'd planned when you started off by having an enjoyable night in? And what sort of a condition are you going to be in for the next twelve hours, calm or short-tempered? Repentant or accusatory? Sociable or violent? Pleasant to be with or a total nightmare?

Worst case scenario is that you are in denial of the amount you have drunk and decide to drive home from a night out. You feel unaffected by all you have consumed over the last few hours and feel invincible. It's not necessary to spell out the consequences of this reckless decision but let it be said, it will affect the lives of many others, not just your own.

On the Wagon

These are just a few of the possible outcomes of not being in control of our actions and fulfilling our responsibilities. Children who grow up in this sort of environment, passively witnessing their parents drink themselves to oblivion every night will not have any respect for them. They will not enjoy their company, so will spend more and more time apart from them, will hide in their rooms for want of remaining safe or to shield themselves from a loud and embarrassing parent, or become reclusive and just prefer to spend time on their own.

Another effect on the child of this anti-social behaviour is that he or she might begin to think this is the right way to behave. He might experiment with alcohol left around the house at far too young an age, form an addiction himself and emulate the abrupt and aggressive manner in which an alcoholic communicates with others, believing it to be the norm.

Learning the basic fundamentals of right and wrong is part of the developmental process. Acting in an appropriate way is then reinforced by our parents or caregivers by means of praise, a slap on the back or even just a smile. As a small child we soon pick up on the things which others like us to do. Why then, when we are older, supposedly fully mature adults, do we regress to infancy and forget these monumentally important facts? We seem to forget our morals, how over-indulgence in anything is wrong and avaricious and how when we have no will power to stop, we carry on and ruin our lives. Are we such weak human beings that we don't have any power over our actions and merely succumb at the first sign of encouragement? The answer is no. We *do* have the power and control over our actions and if we drink to excess, it is absolutely no one else's fault but our own. No one is making you do it other than yourself. They are not pointing a gun at your head, tying you up and using a funnel to pour it down your throat, nor forcing it intravenously through your veins.

The important thing to do, before you try and cut down or cut out your drinking altogether, is to acknowledge that you do have a problem, that you are personally responsible for causing it, that you *can* do something about it and eventually you will be glad that you took the initiative and took responsibility for your own and others' well-being and happiness.

On the Wagon

Chapter 1 – Definitions and Etymology; History of Alcohol

Finding an adequate definition for alcoholism has created much difficulty and controversy for professionals over the years. How much and how often we can drink safely before it causes us problems is significantly a subjective matter, as we all react differently to drugs, alcohol being amongst them.

Neither is there an all-enveloping definition of an alcoholic. The descriptive noun has changed many times over the past, in order to avoid stigma, labelling and erroneous finger pointing. Whatever the noun used however, it is irrefutable that we all know the type of person to whom we refer – a person who is addicted to alcoholic beverages and who consistently drinks to excess, to the detriment of their own health, who fails to fulfil their responsibilities owing to this addiction and who jeopardises the safety and well-being of others in the process.

Alcoholism has a number of negative connotations and these definitions have included such descriptions as: addiction, greed, avarice, maladaptive behaviour, alcohol misuse, abuse and dependence, all terms which hint at the inability to consume drink in moderation and which are associated with obsession and which fall on the boundaries of mental illness. Some terms such as *disease* imply little involvement from the alcoholic themselves, although in reality we are all responsible for our own actions and no one forces us to consume great quantities of alcohol other than ourselves. The term disease is controversial but the condition does follow the same course of progression: one drinks, one continues to drink, the condition worsens, harmful consequences result, affecting one's life, physically, mentally, emotionally and also socially. It is interesting to note that Bill W., co-founder of Alcoholics Anonymous (and who prefers his surname not to be disclosed either), similarly refers to the condition as an illness or *malady*, suggesting that the series of events happens totally against our will.

In the 19th and early 20th Century, the addiction was referred to as *dipsomania*, the irresistible urge to drink alcohol, although in the present day, the term *alcohol dependence syndrome* is preferred (WHO, 1979) to refer to the 140 million people worldwide who suffer from this affliction. Whether this rather lengthy and highfalutin description will endure over time is doubtful but for now the professionals opt to use it. The word *alcoholism* has been used consistently throughout this book however, for the purposes of simplicity, brevity and mainly because it is the phrase still used by the majority in everyday society.

The source referred to for any official definition of addictive behaviour, is the Diagnostic Statistical Manual. Currently on its fifth edition (DSM-V), the Manual suggests that a problem with alcohol exists when a person yielding to recurrent alcohol

On the Wagon

use fails to fulfill their obligations and their behaviour consequently results in physically hazardous situations, social or interpersonal problems, legal problems and/or reckless or dangerous situations. The only issue with this sort of definition is that excessive drinking can continue for a considerable amount of time without diagnosis and indeed well before any of these circumstances materialise. The hardened drinker may be drinking alone and in some clandestine location without detection or the intervention of anyone else for a long period of time. Alternatively, someone else may be keeping the secret for the alcoholic in fear of reprisal or other negative outcome, for example the possibility that their children may be taken into care by welfare personnel of social services, should the condition become public knowledge.

So, how much is it safe to drink without becoming dependent? There is no definite criteria for 'safe' drinking although The Dietary Guidelines for Americans and the National Institute on Alcohol Abuse and Alcoholism (NIAAA) (1995), suggest that *moderate drinking* is no more than two alcohol beverages per day (for men) and one (for women). Those over 65 should not exceed an average of one drink per day, or three on any one occasion. More than fourteen for men and seven for women and those over 65, per week, would infer at least hazardous drinking. The limitations of this sort of recommendation of course wholly depend on the alcoholic content of the specific drink consumed and the size of the glass!

There are those who drink every day and who are never very far away from an alcoholic drink. Their life is organised in such a way that actions are carried out with the next drink in mind, rather than having a drink when all that they need to do has been done. They know where their next drink is coming from and feel safe in the knowledge that it awaits them in the fridge or the drawer of their desk. This is the type of person most at risk as they regularly exceed safe drinking recommendations and will invariably be affecting their health already in the process.

Binge drinking conversely, can be defined as the consumption of four or more alcoholic drinks on any one occasion in the case of women and five or more for men. Although binge drinkers are not usually alcohol dependent, their intermittent but excessive drinking habits account for a great majority of national alcohol-related economic costs. This type of drinking is very popular with younger people who don't drink all week but then who drink all they can at the weekend or when on holiday. As they do not regularly consume alcohol, their bodies are rarely able to handle the excessive amounts they drink all in one go and that is why, when walking through the town late at night on a Friday or Saturday night, many youngsters are seen staggering about with their friends' arms around them for stability, vomiting on the pavement or else totally paralytic on some park bench or street corner.

On the Wagon

Nowadays by law, producers of alcoholic drinks must display the alcohol content of the liquid on the label. You will see however that even a bottle of wine can vary in percentage rating from a low 9% right up to a daunting 16%. Beers can range from a 2% to a 12%, the two being particularly weak and anything above a 6% being an extremely strong, often locally brewed ale. Taste alone however is not a sufficient clue to a drink's potency. If the product's label isn't enough to baffle you, the algebra required to calculate the ABV (alcohol by volume) is sure to do so. ABV standards are used worldwide to measure the amount of ethanol in any one alcoholic beverage. The ABV is the quantity of ethanol (in millilitres) present in every 100 ml of the solution, divided by its density at 20°C.

A good source for determining the alcohol content of your favourite tipple and working out how much you can safely drink on a night out, can be found at the following website: http://www.alcoholcontents.com/

It may be disconcerting to learn that even fruit juices contain some naturally occurring ABV, but this is an insignificant amount and nothing compared to drinks such as Absinthe (up to 89.9%), and some neutral grain and rectified spirits which can contain over 90% alcohol. You may as well drink methylated spirits when you reach this level of alcohol and these are not the sort of drinks you want to be drinking if you have to get up at 7 am in the morning, or even if you want to get up at all!

Body size and weight of the individual are determinants not often considered when considering how much we can safely drink. It does however go without saying that a size zero female on a binge drinking night out will not be able to keep pace with a twenty stone rugby player who regularly downs high levels of strong alcohol.

There are significant individual differences when it comes to the quantity of alcohol consumed before negative effects are experienced. People's reactions vary significantly and are influenced by such factors as their age, gender, their fitness level, weight, how much food they consumed prior to drinking, whether they are taking any form of medication or other drugs, besides how quickly and over what period of time they drank the alcohol.

Countries impose their own laws regarding the age at which it becomes legal to drink for a good reason. In the UK, the official age is eighteen although most teenagers have at least sampled alcohol before the age of sixteen. According to the Government's chief medical officer, Sir Liam Donaldson, alcohol can seriously damage the brains of minors. If they drink under fifteen years of age for example, whilst their brains are still developing, irreparable damage can occur. In the 1960s and 70s, children were told that if they drank before their sixteenth birthday their stomachs would not be able to cope and they would vomit as a result. Whether you actually damage your stomach by drinking at this age is debatable but parents were already aware of the consequences and that the stomach would be the first part of their child's body which would be affected by prematurely consumed alcohol and thus gave the warning to denounce responsibility of having to clear up their child's inexpertly-aimed vomit around the home.

Alcohol has been around since time immemorial and even though we don't know exact dates, it was probably concocted as a result of some fortuitous mixing of ageing berries or honey, left to ferment in the heat. Clear and irrefutable evidence has been found however that it was used as far back as the Stone Age. Beer jugs found by archaeologists show that beverages were fermented intentionally for consumption as far back as the Neolithic period (circa 10,000 B.C.) Not only used as a pleasurable and nutritional drink, alcohol has played an important role in anaesthesia, for numbing the senses when gangrenous bodily parts had to be removed, when a tooth had to be pulled and as an antiseptic on gaping wounds following a battle or accident. Egyptian hieroglyphics drawn on papyrus dating back to around 4000 B.C. similarly depict scenes of wine drinking and all the shenanigans which went along with its consumption.

In many religions, alcohol was, and in some cases still is, widely used during worship. References are made to alcohol in the Old Testament of the Bible, for example when Noah planted a vineyard on Mt Ararat, now eastern Turkey (Genesis 9:20). There are numerous gods signifying alcohol, for example the Babylonians worshiped a wine goddess around the time of 2700 BC, the Ancient Egyptians worshipped Osiris, believed to be the important god that invented beer and the dead were regularly buried in tombs alongside alcoholic beverages for their use in the after-life. They did however warn that the substance should always be taken in moderation and advised against going to taverns, which often doubled up as brothels (Lutz, 1922, pp. 97,105-108). In Ancient China, evidence suggests that people always drank when conducting a religious ceremony, whilst making sacrificial offerings to their gods or ancestors, before entering into battle, celebrating victories, before executions, whilst taking an oath of allegiance, attending a ceremony of birth, marriage, departure, arrival, death, and whatever other occasion equated to a date of significance (Hucker, 1975). In addition, the Chinese have always been very keen on making alcohol available to their guests as a gesture of hospitality, to help them reflect on life and as an antidote for fatigue.

The Greeks formed the cult of Dionysus, which asserted that intoxication brought the people closer to their deity. Ironically this is most certainly the case, as those that drink to excess are inevitably much quicker to meet their maker and therefore enjoy much shorter lives as a result.

On the Wagon

In almost every country and in every walk of life, alcohol has played an important role in people's lives. Cave drawings clearly depict images of people's drinking habits and the sort of receptacles they drank from, recipes of alcoholic beverages have been found on clay tablets and inform us that grapes and berries were used many thousands of years ago, and modern day chemical analysis supports the view that beer made up a great part of the staple diet during Roman times. In fact it is thought that beer may have preceded bread in this manner.

Interestingly, documents still exist from the Middle Ages, to suggest that even nuns had an allowance of six pints of ale each per day. Admittedly in those days, water hygiene was an issue and had to be boiled before it was safe enough to drink but nevertheless, it is surprising to note that kings and ordinary townsfolk alike commonly drank alcohol in order to survive. During this era, monasteries became the principal repositories for beer and wine making, with the monks keeping their carefully guarded techniques firmly under their habits.

There are many allusions to alcohol in great literary works, in fact Shakespeare makes some kind of reference to it in each and every one of his thirty-eight plays. Even the most novice of reader of Shakespeare's plays will know that the objectionable but humorous Sir John Falstaff was very partial to sack (a fortified wine from mainland Spain and the Canary Islands) and often sat intoxicated in taverns, expounding the virtues of the wondrous liquor. He had a particular favourite, a tipple known as *sherris sack*, a fortified wine produced in Jerez de la Frontera (mainland Spain, in the Province of Cádiz). Falstaff believed this drink was capable of clearing the brain, warming the soul and giving a man great courage.

Many modern day works similarly use references to the drinking of alcohol particularly as a precursor to love making scenes. In *Fifty Shades of Grey,* the poor deluded Anastasia has to be continually under the influence before she can endure the sadistic degradation and kinky spankings of Christian Grey, although it is questionable if the verbose and lewd ramblings of E. L. James could extend to anything more original used in foreplay than a couple of glasses of Chardonnay. More impressive to the discerning reader, are the books by Ken Follett, who can write a masterly scene of seduction following a tipple of the hard stuff and who can admirably succeed in making the reader believe they are actually experiencing the heightened pleasures for themselves (Eye of the Needle, Pillars of the Earth, A World Without End etc.)

Many films attempt to offer a realistic glimpse into the life of an alcoholic although some portray this aspect better than others. Here are some which come to mind when considering the depiction of drunks: *Tyrannosaur, Strange Brew, Bad Santa, Days of Wine and Roses, Flight, The Lost Weekend, Arthur, Under the Volcano* and *Leaving Las Vegas.*

On the Wagon

Whether we like it or not, alcohol is here to stay. Its long history gives evidence of this. The concern is for those who have to rule it out of their present lives for various reasons as it will always be around us, whether advertised on TV during the commercials or in plain sight in supermarkets, in every bar and most restaurants throughout the world.

Chapter 2 – Known causes of alcohol dependence and early warning signs

There are a thousand and one reasons why we might drink, certainly too many to mention here but under normal circumstances we might drink to elevate our mood, to celebrate a happy occasion, to prolong the enjoyment of our time spent in good company and to help us relax and wind down after a hard week's work. We drink to be sociable, to reduce our anxieties and to revel in a period spent in a stress-free environment.

Besides drinking solely for pleasure, alcohol consumption is used for many other purposes. Whilst inebriated, we are able to temporarily forget for example about bereavement, occupational stress, health concerns, financial worries and relationship problems. We often overlook however that pre-existing issues like these can be escaped for a while in this way but the numbing effects of alcohol can only help in the short-term and problems will not miraculously disappear overnight. This is an ineffective approach to deal with life's problems. It is far better to deal with the stressors in life as they rear their ugly head, allowing time to celebrate later, when each problem has been dealt with appropriately.

Some people drink to help them sleep. If they can't sleep because they have an unresolved problem, the same as above applies. It needs to be dealt with, as it won't simply vanish into thin air. Alcohol it is true, does help you to sleep. It is a depressant – a sedative which dampens down the activity of neurons in the central nervous system. On the negative side, if taken in sufficiently great proportions, it will prevent you waking up at all! If however you rely on it for helping you to get to sleep in the first place, you will inevitably find that a few hours later on you are suffering from insomnia and ironically you wake during the night or far too early to have provided yourself with a good night's rest. Drowsiness effects will have worn off, so despite the fact you still want to sleep, your neurons will have become excited again and want to party!

Another reason people drink is because their friends do. Whether you are twelve, twenty-two or sixty-two, the effects of peer pressure are equally as powerful and compelling. As teenagers first experiment with alcohol, their primary introduction to the stuff will be the abandoned dregs from bottles their parents have long forgotten about, or cans of beer squirrelled away when they pray their dads were too drunk (or just too inept) to keep an accurate tally on the contents of the fridge. From personal experience, I remember filling an old hip flask with some disgusting tasting ten year old vermouth, the remainder of which ended up in my dad's car as screen wash fluid. Groups of children are regularly spotted on local parks, taking it in turns to swig from bottles, semi-concealed in Tesco carrier bags. The odd thing is that it is more of an initiation test, or rite of passage into a group, than a voluntary act based on enjoyment. You can tell this by the grimaces and contorted faces they pull as they force down every gulp of the despicable fluid. Excitement is gained from the fear of danger elicited by getting caught in the act of underage drinking and yet they draw attention to themselves even more as one after another their heads swivel round and their necks crane to survey the territory to check for anyone approaching, much like an anxious mob of meerkats.

One of the key factors to drinking alcohol is its availability. It is so easy to stop off at the supermarket on the way home from work, or at the local off-license just down the road from where you live. Aisle after aisle of bottles aim to seduce us into picking them up and surreptitiously adding them to our trolley or basket. Under-age children can relatively easily persuade an irresponsible older person to pick them up a can or two from the garage along with their packet of cigarettes, unquestioned by the proprietor. As the availability of food is blamed on the obesity of so many, alcohol similarly lacks the barriers to access in modern-day society. Curiously, in some countries, the cost of a locally-produced beer can be significantly cheaper than a bottle of water. You may think that this explains why so many people become alcoholics but in fact Mediterranean folk might drink during the day but they do not tend to drink to excess. They often make one drink last the full duration of their excessively drawn out mid-afternoon meal, knowing that they will have to drive back to work after their siesta.

Governments continually increase the tax imposed on alcohol but this rarely acts as a successful deterrent to people to cut back on its consumption. Maybe if a 'happy hour' or 'tipsy time' was allotted as the only time during which alcohol could be purchased (outside pubs and bars), surely fewer of us would find ourselves available to buy it at that particular time and so have to forego it.

Those who have other family members with a positive history of alcoholism, exhibit a greater number of factors which contribute towards the predisposition of that, and other addictive behaviours. Studies of individuals' neurotransmitter systems indicate a greater likelihood towards dependence and craving of alcohol and narcotics (Chick et al., 2004). Whether they have a father, grandfather or older brother who regularly drinks to excess, adolescence is a vulnerable period during which many youngsters will try their first alcoholic drink and experiment with different concoctions. They are unaware of the effects, particularly when several types of drink are consumed on the same day. A wise old saying used to advise against drinking beer on the same evening as wine:

The hop and the vine should never entwine!

On the Wagon

Many other sayings have appeared nowadays although it is doubtful if they have been proven scientifically. There does however seem to be a general consensus about not mixing your drinks:

Beer to whiskey, always risky.
Whiskey to beer, never fear.

Beer before wine you'll be fine
Wine before beer, you'll feel queer!!

Mix dark with light and you'll puke all night

Liquor before beer, you're in the clear. Beer before liquor, never been sicker!

Other rhymes advise about the unavoidable consequences of too much alcohol:

Whisky makes you frisky,
Brandy makes you randy

Liquor in the front
Poker in the rear.

Totally confusing and mind-boggling too, these questionable words of wisdom have become distorted over time but, from personal experience and others' too, the mixing of drinks is wholly discouraged. Here are a few of those not to be tampered with: beer and cider, wine and beer (in whichever order!), vodka and Calvados and wine and absinthe. The latter incidentally would seem to contain hallucinogens and you *will* be saying and doing things later which will be regretted and which come back to haunt you later, without a doubt!

Having said all this, adolescents will inevitably make up their own minds and hopefully learn quickly from their mistakes. Luckily most teenagers abhor the taste of any alcohol whatsoever and this mode of thinking should be prolonged and encouraged for as long as possible. After even just a small quantity of alcohol, everyone will appear to be in a good mood, those normally nervous and self-conscious teenagers will now lose their inhibitions and become uncharacteristically sociable. On the negative side, the alcohol will make them feel invincible and exceptionally daring. This is a big worry for parents as, in addition to not always being told where their child is at this age, the adolescent could well be acting irresponsibly and without concern for their own safety or that of others. A thirst for adventure and perilous pursuits can lead to trouble for the thrill-seeking adolescent, particularly as it is also around this time that they often learn to drive. The novice driver with their newly acquired 'skills' is not yet aware of or mentally prepared for the other lackadaisical or reckless drivers on the road and this does not fare well for them, their passengers or anyone else on the roads at this time.

On the Wagon

Promiscuity also goes hand in hand with the experimentation of alcohol and this is when we hope parental and school teachings about the birds and the bees have been heeded and that the advice of carrying a rain jacket in case of a storm has been adequately digested.

Gender differences exist in relation to levels of tolerance of alcohol. For example women are more vulnerable to the adverse effects of drinking too much. Even if a male and female weigh the same amount and drink an equivalent quantity, the female tends to carry less bodily water and will therefore have greater concentrations of the alcohol present in her blood. Females also have less *dehydrogenase* in their stomach, the enzyme which breaks down alcohol and could mean absorption of up to a third more alcohol in her bloodstream than the male. As the evening progresses, many gender specific differences can be noted distinguishing the effects of alcohol tolerance, one of which is in the way the female becomes less reticent and the male becomes more gregarious and frequently loud. Equally susceptible to speech slurring, the female is however more likely to become emotional when she has drunk too much, whereas the male is more likely to continue drinking until he falls fast asleep. Evidence shows however that males consistently consume more alcohol and experience more severe alcohol-related problems than their female counterparts (Substance Abuse and Mental Health Services Administration, 2008).

As the partner, parent, child or merely a friend of someone who we suspect is drinking to excess, there are early warning signs to notice. Careful consideration should be made however before coming to a potentially wrong conclusion. Alcoholics are incredibly defensive about their addiction and will do all they can to disprove any ill-timed incriminations. You may also lose their trust and friendship in the process, so be very sure of your facts before jumping in to offer your expert help.

If you know the person particularly well, the first thing you may notice is their increasing secrecy. On your sudden appearance into the same room, they may move or hide something rapidly, out of your sight. Even though they might drink sociably with you in public, an additional quantity of alcohol will be needed to supplement this consumption with more at home (at work or at school). The best thing you can do is to pretend you haven't noticed and to choose an appropriate time afterwards, without fear of being caught, to check up on their secret bottle hoard. A word of warning, this hidden cache might not be the only one. As the alcoholic gets more accomplished at this new-found deception, they may try to fool you by having several, separate hiding places for their treasured stash. The deception becomes like a game to the alcoholic, he will get more daring with this and even drink out in public, disguising home-made wine, for example, in a cordial bottle. He will also start to carry chewing gum or a breath freshener to prevent being found out by his peers or colleagues.

On the Wagon

If the regular shopping trip is something you do together, make a mental note of the amount of alcohol which is being purchased, whether more time is spent on choosing the alcohol and whether the overall amount spent on it is gradually increasing. These are factors which even the most conscientious drinker will not be able to conceal. He or she may however discretely try to obscure some of the bottles or cans in the trolley with other, more mundane purchases. Once again, do not jump to conclusions. Maybe there is some rationale behind the extra cans this week – a barbeque at the weekend, a few days off work coming up, or some friends coming round who they might want to impress?

Check abandoned receipts for additional alcohol purchases. In addition to the weekly allotted quota spent at the supermarket, has more been bought randomly from elsewhere? These actions all sound rather devious and underhand but you have their best interests to heart and at the top of your agenda, right?

Chapter 3 – Physical and Psychological Effects and other consequences

As the allotted drinking time approaches, we might get a little edgy and excited in anticipation of the good time ahead but also slightly fretful that something might interrupt, or worst still, prevent us from enjoying our much prized drinking session. Neurotransmitters in our brain interact with the behavioural reinforcement which we receive when we participate in hedonistic experiences and subsequently nurture a response mechanism making it more likely that we crave that pleasant feeling again. Unfortunately it's this very response of repeatedly seeking pleasure that elicits the addictive or dependence craving. In other words, because we enjoy the alcohol and its euphoric effects so much, we self-perpetuate this action by trying to attain this state more often until we build up a tolerance, finally having to consume more and more alcohol to gain this desired state of mind.

Luckily the majority of us do not suffer to any great degree from the effects of an evening spent drinking, other than perhaps for the occasional hangover or slight drowsiness the next day. Others though, may become one of the 7.4% of the population who suffer from alcohol abuse and who meet the statistical criteria for dependence on this type of drug. According to the National Council on Alcoholism and Drug Dependence, Inc. (NCADD), alcoholism is the greatest health concern for society in the United States of America with national expenses on this far exceeding money spent on cancer, obesity or diabetes. Dependence on alcohol can put enormous strain on the financial economy, health care and judicial systems, in addition to all the worry placed on those people who might be affected by someone's excessive drinking habits. The addiction affects 17.6 million people in America, a huge increase from the 14 million reported in 2000 (Rockville, M.D., 2000).

Shockingly, alcohol accounts for 73% of the more serious offences, in particular child beating, rape, wife battering, stabbings and murders, clearly demonstrating that many people are beyond control of their own actions whilst under the influence of intoxicating drinks.

There is no doubt that most people enjoy a drink but to drink in moderation and to stay within the limits of the law is quite necessary. Without such limits being imposed on ourselves, many psychological problems will be experienced that previously we did not possess. Along with excessive drinking comes depression. When alcohol becomes the primary focus in life, the state of euphoria cannot be maintained and therefore, as the effects of the alcohol wear off, we experience a low, a period of negative thoughts, feelings of inertia and lack of caring.

Any kind of addiction is a brain disorder, characterised by compulsive involvement with the source of the addiction, whether this is drugs, alcohol, or

On the Wagon

smoking. The individual will continue to seek the source disregarding its hold on him and its harmful consequences. Alcohol is one of the types of addiction which causes chronic chemical changes in the brain, which affect a person's ability to think clearly, behave with decorum or even feel normal without partaking in the activity. The addiction leads to tolerance, a need for more and more of the substance in order to experience the same heightened feelings as before. To give up the addiction often incurs withdrawal symptoms and a weakness of resolve after periods of abstinence, increasing the likelihood of relapse.

The longer the dependence lasts, the less inclined the alcoholic is to work. In fact the drink makes him or her quite incapable of holding down a regular job. The habit can be so severe that the money situation becomes very tight, until all one's earnings are spent on alcohol leaving nothing for household expenses and other necessary outgoings. The inability to work plus the undesirability of the person as an employee can lead to destitution and sometimes a person will even have to sleep rough as he finds he has nothing left in life.

Alcoholics become very defensive of the things and people they have in their lives. Instead of showing their loved ones affection as they did in the past, they can no longer treat them with respect and become volatile, angry and abrupt. furthermore they display jealousy towards their partner for having friends outside the home and even towards their own child for enjoying life as they can no longer find enjoyment themselves without a full bottle at their side. This jealousy may turn to paranoia when they suddenly find that members of the household are going out more and more. Ironically it is purely as they have become the person they are now that has encouraged the others to escape the house so often. Beware though, as on returning home, the addict may have had to drown his sorrows and the relief he experiences on the return of the significant other, may be shown in ways of violence as opposed to welcoming signs of affection.

Alcoholics kid themselves that the unhappy state of events is not their fault. They go into denial and will invariably blame others for the way they feel. It is a way of unburdening themselves of the guilt they feel for becoming a poor partner, parent or child. Blame is a major symptom of depression and acts as a defense mechanism to allow the undesirable behaviour to continue.

The person will, behind a façade of superiority, realise that they are in a Catch 22 position, that their life is going nowhere, they cannot afford to change their circumstances and that their relationships are going awry and for this reason they start to become very emotional. Whilst under the influence of alcohol and after the period of initial heightened pleasure, they become melancholic. They start thinking about special and memorable times in the past and about people they have lost or who have

On the Wagon

died, people who strangely now become suddenly incredibly important to them. They may also be somewhat aware of the destruction they are causing in the home and worry about the damage they are doing to relationships, even though this will only last for a short while. However, whilst this lasts, the alcoholic may be extremely tearful and hold on tight to their children and look plaintively at their partner for understanding.

Alcohol has several dire effects on the body, some of which can improve over time if the addict becomes teetotal and others which unfortunately are irreversible. When consumed excessively, alcohol causes our brains to become befuddled, our liver fails to function adequately and our sense of coordination and other sensory-motor processes substantially deteriorate. A dullness of sensation is experienced (i.e. pain and temperature), our thinking is impaired, our sleep patterns are interrupted and, more worryingly, we may suffer a coma or even death (Darley et al, 1984).

Alcohol significantly alters our behaviour. As the drink is consumed, it enters the stomach, allowing 20% of the alcohol to filter through the stomach lining, absorbed directly into the bloodstream. Any remaining alcohol later passes through the small intestine, once again into the bloodstream. This pathway takes the alcohol to the Central Nervous System (CNS), the first effects on which are to alter our judgement and make us less inhibited. The drinker thus becomes more talkative and less self-conscious. However, while some become more relaxed and affable, others become morose and belligerent or aggressive. A personal observation is the initial boundless energy experienced when, after a couple of drinks, there is a perceived capability to clean the entire house. Notice the emphasis here on the word *perceived*!

This paradoxical effect often erroneously leads people to the assumption that alcohol is a stimulant, when in fact it is a CNS depressant. The increased but temporary stimulation or activity is caused by the disinhibition, the dampening down or *depressing* of some regions of the CNS.

The problem with alcohol is that it is not chemically broken down like other things we digest. The liver has to work hard to convert about 90% of it into CO^2 and water, whilst the remainder is released by breathing, perspiring or passing through the body and released as urine. The liver has a limited capability to deal with the alcohol, only able to cope with one third or a half an ounce of alcohol per hour, above this the liver is overworked and with the abuse, problems can ensue. A liver which is severely abused by alcohol, may become enlarged and scarred, known as *cirrhosis*, which can be fatal.

As the quantity of alcohol in the bloodstream builds up, the depressant effect becomes more evident: pain is dulled, speech becomes slurred, co-ordination and reactions are affected and sight becomes blurred. The progression from hyperactivity to calm sedation

On the Wagon

depends on many factors but it is inevitable and undetectable by the drinker himself, making this a particularly dangerous time to get behind the wheel of a car for example.

Effects on our emotions vary most, with one person displaying overtly friendly behaviour while another will be melancholy and incommunicative. The natural personality of the person will have a bearing on this, so a staid individual will be perceived as more outgoing, whereas one who normally suppresses aggressive tendencies may expose a nastier side to them while drinking. Alcohol makes us into people who, in reality, we are not. It has a devilish nature which lurks below the surface of our psyche, ready to make us socially unacceptable, loud, embarrassing, uninhibited and often downright dangerous.

Aggression is one of the worst features of alcoholism. A previously good natured and calm person can be transformed into an evil monster under the influence of a few drinks. Observations have been made during research involving primates that aggression levels are negatively correlated with serotonin levels. The researchers found that monkeys displayed more aggression and caused each other more injuries with reduced serotonin activity in their cerebrospinal fluid. (Higley et al., 1992). Diminished levels of this hormone have similarly been found in aggressive humans: children who are cruel to animals and who are disruptive in class (Kruesi, 1979) and in U.S. Marines punished for untoward violence (Brown et al., 1979). Although it is not always wise to extrapolate the results of primate studies to humans, there is nevertheless some indication that alcohol reduces serotonin in the body and can therefore go some way towards explaining the subsequent aggression associated with alcoholism.

Embarrassing side-effects are associated with excess drinking. With the first couple of drinks comes the feeling that we are suddenly more attractive to others, with subsequent drinks making everyone else seem more attractive to us too. However, the amorous and flirtatious effects of the first couple of drinks soon diminish when the 'one too many' starts to have detrimental effects on your love life, causing loss of libido, erectile and orgasmic dysfunction. The aptly named *Brewer's Droop* is renowned for spoiling many a romantic moment occurring when the depressant effects of the alcohol kick in and prevent the brain communicating effectively with the body. Alcohol will relax the *corpora cavernosa* in the penis which have become swollen with blood but the alcohol in your system keeps your blood vessels and veins open, resulting in the blood draining away, leaving it flaccid and uncooperative.

Shakespeare was obviously conversant with this annoying fact of life when he suggested that alcohol *"provokes the desire but takes away the performance."*

People who become dependent upon alcohol begin to experience unpleasant side effects if they have not had any for a few hours. They might start to shake, sweat profusely and feel listless or tired owing to the sudden drop in the blood's alcohol level.

On the Wagon

Feelings of nausea may ensue followed by uncontrollable vomiting attacks. Anxiety makes their hearts beat faster and their blood pressure rises as a result. They become impatient and easily irritated and in extreme cases, suffer from a type of severe confusion known as the DTs (delirium tremors). Ironically, a person suffering from this symptom may find the strange thoughts and hallucinations similar to those experienced whilst under the influence of some highly potent alcoholic drinks such as Absinthe, which contains wormwood, a powerful hallucinogen.

Chronic alcoholics do not place enough emphasis on healthy dietary requirements, often foregoing regular meals. To them, drinking is all they need to supply them with energy and fulfillment but long-term neglect leaves the person vulnerable to changes in the cerebral structures of the brain. As a result, lesions may occur in the hippocampus, which is located in the temporal cortex. A consequence of this might entail severe loss of memory. Korsakoff syndrome, named after the Russian physician who initially described the disorder, entails patients suffering from Anterograde Amnesia, the inability to form new memories, despite maintaining a thoroughly accurate long-term memory. An often cited case study relevant here is the one of HM, who regularly suffered from epileptic seizures. Medication did not seem to help and at the age of twenty-nine, this young man had surgery performed on him to reduce the seizures. This procedure can have unfortunate side-effects and he suffered a lesion in his hippocampus. He seemed to have recovered after surgery and soon after, his family moved. His long-term memory remained securely intact and lead him home, time after time to his old house but he was unable to remember at any point where the new house was located. He therefore continually got lost. About this time, he was also informed that a favourite uncle of his had died, which caused him extreme distress. Even more sad was, that when he asked (regularly) when his uncle was next due to visit, the family had to inform him yet again that his uncle had died, the effect on the young man was just as potent and upsetting for him as the first time, demonstrating the irreparable damage incurred to his short-term memory. This is one of the horrifying side-effects of chronic alcoholism too.

Elevated blood pressure can occur as a result of chronic excess drinking. It is also a precursor to more serious cardiovascular disease related to alcoholism. Hypertension can however be reversed and blood pressure levels will begin to stabilise on the discontinuation of alcohol consumption

There has always been a strong association between excessive alcohol use and increased cortisol levels. Cortisol is a hormone which is secreted by the adrenal gland. It is secreted to a greater degree when the individual is under stress and over an extended period of time can result in ulcers, fatigue, an impaired immune system, faster deterioration of the brain during ageing and has been known to contribute towards cancer.

On the Wagon

The endocrine system, whose job it is to regulate the hormones of our body and allow the different regions to communicate with each other, can be detrimentally affected by alcohol abuse. This system produces hormones in the hypothalamus, pituitary, thyroid, pancreas and adrenal glands, so plays a very important part in the provision of our health. Resulting effects may include the blocking of absorption of calcium which in turn may incur osteoporosis or brittle bone syndrome. Testosterone levels will decrease leading to erectile dysfunction and cardiovascular problems owing to an imbalance in glucose and lipid levels.

All these unpleasant physiological responses occur as a direct result of drinking, providing us with yet another reason to curb our drinking or better still to abstain altogether. When someone drinks heavily on a regular basis, they need constant medical check-ups and tests carried out to ensure that their health is not deteriorating to such a degree that hospitalisation becomes imperative.

On the Wagon

Chapter 4 - What life might be like to live with someone with alcohol dependency

During the course of my research on alcoholism, I took the opportunity to speak to several people who had either been addicted to alcohol or who had been affected by living with someone who was an alcoholic. One lady, who had a drunk for a father, openly recounted that many of her childhood memories were marred by the family having to organise their lives around the drinking habits of her parent. Huge expenditure on alcohol ruled out any possibility of family vacations and the chances of any social life were significantly affected by having to stay at home to 'dad sit', as her siblings referred to it and ensure that no harm came to her father whilst inebriated. She sadly referred to regular occurrences of excess brandy drinking which would extend long into the evening and inevitably culminate in him becoming so intoxicated that he would pass out, wherever he was at the time. The distressing scenario the lady described was of a large fully-grown man lying comatose on the hall floor. Being tall and of a large girth, the man had been known to block the main entrance and create an impenetrable obstacle to other family members returning to the house. A major fire risk also prevailed, as being an alcoholic did not mix well with also being a smoker. He justified his drinking by asserting that it was the tradition of his country to drink heavily and that all his friends did the same thing. This is just one sad portrayal of how one starts drinking to excess and how it affects everyone around you.

In this chapter, I have included several real-life scenarios offered by those I spoke to. The names of the family members have of course been changed and all other identifying markers removed to retain confidentiality.

When a relationship goes wrong, for whatever reason, you tend to overlook any happy memories as they become clouded by all the bad things which occurred at the time. In my own case however, I still have vivid memories of the good times too – the purchase of our first house, the wedding day, the delight on finding out I was pregnant, all the happy holidays together and even the excitement of running a new business together. They did evoke considerable happiness at the time but, on reflection, it is doubtful if any of these special times would have been particularly enjoyed by my partner without the support of a bottle in close proximity.

The memory of our first date was marred by the fact that cider bottles were hidden under the long leather couch in the pub, to supplement pints of beer purchased at the bar. I was never sure whether this was to avoid escalating pub prices or to save the delays in the crowded queues for the next round of drinks. Our first kiss was a clumsy and unmemorable attempt at co-ordinating the pressing of lips together whilst standing balanced on two feet. The habit did however develop into a pattern whereby extra alcohol accompanied us everywhere. The ten minute walk to the pub in an evening was seemingly too long to wait for a pint served at the bar, a large bottle of pear cider had to be consumed along the way. On arrival to a holiday resort, the first stop after dumping our suitcases in the hotel would be at the local supermarket to stock up on drinks to be consumed before going out for an evening of eating and considerably more drinking. The thrill of having a baby was soon replaced by more excessive drinking to obliterate the annoyance and

On the Wagon

disturbance of crying in the night and any business success was overcast by the need to drink in order to forget the hard work involved, the long days, objectionable customers and lack of profit.

I showed my interest when a new hobby was mentioned … but ironically this turned out to be making home-made wine and beer, which is particularly high in alcohol content. Admittedly the taste was exceptionally good for a cheap kit bought in the local hardware store but there was a downside for my partner. He wouldn't be able to stop at just one glass of wine or even two but would have to consume the equivalent of a whole bottle, then progress on to the home-made beer as well. These evenings would invariably turn out to be a particularly merry time when, as a whole family, we would dance to our favourite music or go for a bike ride (one of the saddle bags brimming over with extra supplies of course) and we would end up at an old pub with a welcoming family garden. This would be fine unless it was mid-winter, when to sit outside with a pint was far from enjoyable. Friends' weddings were alright as there was usually a pre-allotted 'tab' available behind the bar. People cottoned on to the fact that it was best to get your orders in quickly and therefore ridiculously expensive drinks would be selected, purely because they were free for a certain length of time, or until the designated bar tab had been used up. Brandy and Babycham, Snakebites (a lethal concoction of beer and cider mixed), elaborate cocktails and whiskies with all manner of questionable mixers were consumed and then promptly wasted by being regurgitated into the flower beds outside (or on recently polished floors, whichever was located first).

Set days of the week were designated as 'getting pissed up' nights. This was not just intended as a quiet night in with a couple of nice drinks but rather 'I am going to drink myself stupid until I fall into a drunken stupor night'. The amount consumed was actually incredible looking back. I later learned all this was being supplemented by another, disguisable alcoholic drink which was in itself lethal, let alone drunk in conjunction with anything else – vodka. Many a tummy upset in a Spanish resort was blamed on the beachside burger bar when it was far more likely to have been the sheer quantity of alcohol consumed in such a short period of time.

Do any of these experiences seem familiar to you? Were you the one having to run off the beach to sprint back to the hotel before you showed yourself up in public with the remains of last night's prawn paella dripping down your legs? Or perhaps you were the poor person who had to stand by embarrassed, asking the hotel receptionist if you could borrow a mop, bucket and lots of disinfectant? Sounds disgusting, doesn't it, but if they are honest, these are some of the regular occurrences experienced by alcoholics and by those who have to endure the consequences of their drinking habit.

A non-drinking night is ironically far worse as you know quite well that tempers will be frayed and fuses will be short. In fact you do everything within your power to keep the peace. Children will have to forego their after school cartoons as the master drinker will not be able to tolerate such trivial programmes on TV. In fact the remote control is surreptitiously nudged his way to avoid any animosity over preferred channels and it is completely out of the question to suggest a soap opera or even a comedy. Joviality of any sort, laughing, happy chatter, singing or the like are forbidden at this precarious moment of time. Any wrong action or word uttered might result in the pet cat flying through the air on the end of a well-aimed size 10 and everyone else's choice of activity for the evening has long ago slithered out of the proverbial window.

On the Wagon

From this moment on, while the cyclical drink-recover-drink process gathers momentum, life is made hell for the rest of human kind, or at least for the rest of the inhabitants of that one particular household. I say that, as no one else knows about the trouble brewing behind closed doors. How the spouse can't relax as the amorous demands of the drunkard are anticipated, with the emergence of swollen libido which accompanies the heightened provocativeness of the first couple of drinks, then subdues with the consumption of the third and fourth, more intent at this point on welcoming the fifth and sixth. By now the libido has metamorphosed into a shrunken and deflated balloon, whizzing above the room, scoffing and blowing raspberries at the drinker's incapacity to prove its masculinity.

Others are not aware that the children are having part of their childhood taken brutally away from them, prohibited from giggling at the silly little things that normal children do, tiptoeing around so as not to rouse the ogre who has fallen prematurely asleep in a comatose state in front of the TV, and in severe trepidation of informing anyone that help is required with the mathematics homework they haven't quite understood. The whole atmosphere becomes one of fuel-accelerated tension, no one knowing what's going to happen next, who's going to get shouted at, sworn at or used as boxing practice.

Sadly, aggression is one of the seedier sides of alcoholism. The drinker projects his anger and feelings of failure on to another person, ironically often the person or people he loves most:

> I feel like I wasted my 20s and most of my 30s living with an alcoholic. He was either very drunk, planning when he was next going to get drunk or else violent and bad-tempered. I have no doubt at all that he loved me and the children but he thumped me on numerous occasions and punched, pinched and kicked the children with regular occurrence. If he disagreed with me about something, he would call me unmentionable names and would question me every time I spoke to anyone of the opposite sex. He was convinced I was having an affair, which I was not and life became unbearable living with him. Finally I gave him an ultimatum to cut down on his drinking and stop abusing us or I'd leave him. In the end, his violent temper got out of hand and meant that we were compelled to leave, (the children were actually pleading with me) or he'd have caused one of us a serious injury.

This woman did the right thing in this case leaving her husband, the house was no longer a safe and happy place for her or the children. She had given the brute adequate time to contemplate what he was doing wrong and had failed in her attempt to get outside help. It transpires that her own GP, when she went to see him covered in bruises on her neck and chest, had chosen to ignore the undeniable signs of violence and had not been willing to offer any suggestion other than to make another appointment for both her and her husband to talk to him together on another occasion. This was not a wise suggestion as she would have incurred the wrath of her

On the Wagon

husband for having 'grassed him up' and all hell would have let loose. Instead, she confided in close friends, all of whom told her in no uncertain terms to "get out" and to "dump the b#stard". Finally, close to desperation, she found a solicitor who specialised in matrimonial discord and who advised her exactly the same, to "get out while you still can". A few phone calls later, she and her children were placed in 'safe' housing and were starting to establish a new life together in a new area. As the innocent victim of domestic violence, she was entitled to the house and all its contents but apparently she couldn't bear the thought of living in that house any longer and chose to forego all that reminded her of her previous life.

> *I used to dread going home from work some days. The pretty young woman I had married just five years since had been consumed by drink and was now incapable of holding down a job or of even looking after our little boys. To an outsider, the lovely smile she gave me on my return would have suggested that our life together was perfect but it was far from it. I left work very tired most days from a busy job and then had to commute some eighty miles home. [Jennifer] would be sitting in the garden, laughing and joking with a neighbour over a bottle of wine. The boys would be holding their tummies or crying with hunger but she didn't seem to notice. Empty bottles lined the mantelpiece in the sitting room and half-drunk glasses could be found discarded in the kitchen and even in the bathroom. She had obviously lost them in her drunken forgetfulness and had poured yet another. Despite my exhaustion, I would begin to make the evening meal, while handing my boys a biscuit or a handful of raisins to tide them over for a while. Dirty breakfast bowls were still in the sink, a pile of abandoned clothes sat in front of the washing machine, never having quite made it to the wash cycle. It was extremely depressing to think how one person's selfish actions could affect the whole family and I dare say she was not going to react well to news of the appointment I had made us both with the Marriage Counselling people for the following Monday morning!*

When children are living in the same house as an alcoholic, it may have detrimental effects on their school work, disrupt their sleep patterns, mould their own behaviour and generally have a negative effect on them. In this case, the alcoholic would be completely unreasonable to continue her anti-social behaviour and should be more determined than ever to seek help.

It is foolhardy to build any new friendships outside the home with this turmoil underway. One of the side effects of chronic drinking is paranoia and the drinker will inevitably come to erroneous conclusions if the new friend is any other than the same sex as the spouse. Even simple coffee mornings are spoilt by the ensuing interrogations, the anxious alcoholic wheedling information to ensure their secret is still safe behind the four walls of your house.

Here is another anonymous scenario from someone who lived with an alcoholic:

> *I used to hate the nights when (Greg) got drunk. He would start off all lovey-dovey and affectionate with his first couple of drinks but then, if I hadn't already acquiesced to his sexual advances, he would call me all sorts of names and push me around until I was made to feel there*

On the Wagon

was something wrong with me if I didn't let him have his way with me. One evening, on which I knew he would be drinking, as I had seen him transfer a lot of alcohol to the fridge, I arranged to go out with a few friends and so I put the children to bed before I went out. He didn't seem to mind at all (other than for a jokey threat to stay away from other men). I had a great evening out with my female friends and at midnight it was time to come home by taxi, as arranged. A couple of the girls did not seem to want to leave the dancefloor as their favourite line-dancing song had just come on and so the taxi we had ordered came and then drove off with other customers, as we were taking too long. When we finally got into a taxi, it became evident that we all lived some way away from each other and I was placed second last in the order of drop offs. Well, I arrived home about an hour later than I had told Greg (about 01:15) and I entered the house as quietly as I could, thinking he might be asleep by now. Only he wasn't asleep …but very, very drunk. Without speaking to me or even waiting for an explanation to my tardiness, he thumped me hard in the shoulder and then the stomach, knocking all the wind out of me and I fell to the floor. He then continued to kick me three or four times, shouting all sorts of horrible names to me, until the children appeared at the top of the stairs crying their hearts out, seeing their parents acting like this. At this point, he finally stopped hurting me and went back into the sitting room, shouting upstairs to the children that I was a whore and that I should go and sleep out on the street. I managed to get up and, pretending to my children that I was quite alright, calmed them down and tucked them back into bed. Then I closed myself in the bathroom and cried until I could cry no more.

Events like this are commonplace in the homes of an alcoholic and sadly, it is only the people who live within those four walls who are often aware of the goings on there. Victims of alcohol abuse, such as the one in the case above, do not often reveal their distress or try and seek help, for fear of reprisal and to give further ammunition for violence.

Those living with an alcoholic are often a group neglected by society. Their dilemma is after all unbeknown in the majority of cases. No one wants to broadcast that their partner, parent or even child is an alcoholic and for this reason, many have to live with the consequences and handle the situation single-handedly.

Another, often neglected issue associated with alcoholism, is sexual deviance. This is another scenario, proferred by someone who could no longer endure the unnecessarily uninhibited behaviour of her boyfriend in public places:

I hadn't been with him long at all when he told me that I had to do [it] with him. I had always wanted the first time to be very special and with the person I wanted to spend my life with and I had not yet made up my mind for sure about (Geoff). He often got very drunk and I worried that he would soon forget about me and move on to someone else. I felt coerced by him but eventually gave in. After that, he pressurized me more, making me do it in public places, like the local park late at night, in other people's gardens or bathrooms at friends' parties, round the back of the community centre and even in our local cemetery. When we had been together for some time, I went on holiday with him and he got drunk every night. He would insist on taking lots of photos of me, first showing just my bare legs or a bit of cleavage but later on of me standing in public places totally naked. It embarrassed me no end as I always worried than someone would come along and see me but he said he would keep a look out and he was always nice to me afterwards.

On the Wagon

Occasionally, he'd place the camera at unusual angles, taking pictures of me standing or sitting in uncomfortable postures but it seemed to please him greatly and I thought that he would just delete them soon after. One day, while using his computer because mine had broken, I notice a folder on his desktop with my name on. Obviously I had to see what it contained and was horrified to find those pictures, along with the comments of his friends and similar pictures of their girlfriends. I have never discussed this with him to this day. I deleted all of the photos and walked out, never to see him again.

Not everyone living with an alcoholic decides to leave them to start a new life elsewhere. In fact, in some cases, and in a previously stable relationship, the drinker and his or her partner can work together to solve their problems and successfully achieve sobriety. It is a decision not to be taken lightly but one in which couples can become even closer and their relationships become much stronger than ever. If you have someone you wish to help, or plan on giving up drink on your own but do not know of ways in which you can succeed in this, Chapter 5 will discuss some of the methods used nowadays in helping someone overcome their dependency on alcohol.

On the Wagon

Chapter 5 – Treating Alcoholism

If you have reached a stage with your drinking where you are resolute in your decision to take action and to cut down or to completely abstain, you first have to make sure you **acknowledge** that there *is* a problem. Whether you have noticed you have a decline in health, are no longer able to sustain the expense of the habit or have received an ultimatum from your partner that you must do something about your drinking, it is vital that you personally take on the responsibility of your actions from this point forward.

The first and most important step is to divulge your hitherto darkly-kept secret to at least one other understanding human being. Many people find that their nearest and dearest are the last people they would consider to discuss the matter with at this early stage as they can be the most critical (and the ones who most want you to stop drinking for their own personal reasons). Let's face it, they are often the ones partially blamed for the situation in the first place and to openly confess to them would be downright humiliating and would not help in the slightest. This is probably an erroneous assumption but if you are to stand any chance of handling this momentous decision at all, it is advisable to choose someone who will both sympathise with your situation and who will guide you to take the right course of action, given your unique set of circumstances. This individual should be trusted to be discrete and an ideal person to **confide** in would be one who has experienced an addiction of some sort themselves and overcome it with at least some modicum of success. Don't just blurt it out to your friends in the pub on a Friday evening. Your revelation will be the nub of jokes with them for ever more. You must think this through wisely and not choose someone who could be disloyal to you and make matters worse. There is the kind of person who will light a cigarette and blow smoke in your face when they learn you plan to give up smoking. These are not true friends at all, even if they do find the situation hilariously funny. Remember, the hardest part in taking action against a drinking problem is to admit you actually have a problem – primarily to yourself and then to another discrete individual.

The fear of telling someone else is often the reason why so many alcoholics at this point opt to go along to **Alcoholics Anonymous** (AA) meetings. As its name suggests, the group swears to a code of secrecy and the members who attend do so to support each other through the various stages of abstinence. These groups work along the same lines as a dieting club. It is extremely hard for some people to lose weight if their will-power is not great. Perhaps one's enjoyment of food outweighs the incentives to lose weight and when there is little or no encouragement from those at home to persevere, and no positive feedback when you've been working so hard at cutting down on the calories, you are more likely to slip into old ways and lose your

On the Wagon

resolve. Going along to a club however, run by and attended by similarly-minded individuals all in the same boat, determined to improve their health and well-being, means that you stand a much greater chance of succeeding. Although the efficacy of AA has not been studied under controlled clinical conditions, many believe its beneficial effects can be attributed, to some degree, to the substitution of one's regular drinking partners with a fellowship of AA members, all of whom share the superordinate goal of maintaining abstinence and enjoying life without those consistent cravings for alcohol. Modern studies have found however that a combination of professional treatment and the help of AA, achieves better results than that of AA alone (N.I.A.A.A., 2000). Members of AA consider alcoholism as a lifelong physiological problem rather than an over indulgence or psychological problem. They therefore recommend total abstinence as the only solution. This method is not the ideal answer for all alcoholics but overall, its popularity speaks for itself.

You should also seek help from a professional. Your **local general practitioner** is the ideal first person in whom to confide, as he or she will be able to arrange an appointment for a specialist consultation whilst maintaining confidentiality. If the appointment is then arranged through the National Health system, this should not cost you anything and is highly recommended. Your local GP might appear a little abrupt or uncaring at the surgery or health centre but they do not specialise in this particular problem and are what their job title suggests, a *general* practitioner. Expect them to consider your problem as self-inflicted and to offer you little or no sympathy. This however is an important first port of call and the doctor should have the wherewithal to get you in touch with the right people to help you through what, can only be described as, a potentially difficult time. Whoever you select as the first person in whom you confide your drinking problem, this is the first and most significant step you can make to turn your life around and change things for the better.

If you are conversely intending to help someone else with an excessive drinking problem, it is very important to encourage them to seek professional help. If they do not want to take the appropriate course of action themselves, they will no doubt soon be heading back through the revolving door of recidivism and drinking themselves to oblivion. Persuading an alcoholic to seek professional help is imperative and must be done diplomatically and with the assurance that you only want the best for this person and have no selfish agenda in persuading them to do this.

It might surprise you to know that there are also special groups available for those struggling to live with a loved one's drinking habits as well as for the alcoholic himself. These poor people often get overlooked as these problems usually centre around the health, moods and consequences of the drinker's dubious behaviour. Al-anon is one of these such groups and is a programme intended for those seeking support for the care of alcoholics.

On the Wagon

There are **other groups** available too, like MADD (Mothers Against Drunk Drivers), SADD (Students Against Drunk Drivers), or you could alternatively approach your local council who often have a group of staff specially trained to deal with queries relating to alcoholism and its consequences, for example drinking with excessive measures of alcohol in the blood.

Although most treatments for alcohol dependence will involve a private one-to-one consultation with a therapist, popularity is growing steadily for **group therapy**. This option is more time efficient for the therapist, who can see more than one client at a time and be able to pass on the resultant savings to his clients. This type of therapy is beneficial as the focus of discussion is not concentrated solely on one person and alleviates some of the embarrassment and shame felt by the self-confessing addict. Furthermore it gives the client opportunity to contemplate his own situation by having the opportunity to observe and listen to others.

Group sessions may consist of a group of total strangers or involve family members of the alcoholic. **Family therapy** focuses on communication problems and tries to help ease the disharmonious relationships which have caused the excess drinking in the first place or which have alternatively come about as a result of it. It works in the same way as marriage counselling and aims to make each family member realise they will all be happier if they act as part of a team, working towards the same goal, in this case the goal being to eliminate the cause for the drinking. The alcoholic should find it much easier to abstain when he or she feels they have the support of their loved ones. The only downside of this therapy is that sometimes an alcoholic finds it easier to be more open with complete strangers than those familiar and close, and that is why so many opt for the help of a group like Alcoholics Anonymous.

Some advocate the Learning Model of Therapy. This model believes that maladaptive behaviours are brought about by a faulty way of learning. Therefore to drink to excess is our fault as perhaps we have become too greedy and are over-indulging ourselves because we like the positive effects of drinking so much. The type of therapy recommended for this 'defective' way of thinking would involve *un*-learning the wrongful behaviour. One appropriate example of this would be in **Aversion therapy**:

The one time Irish Manchester United winger and European Footballer of the Year of 1968, George Best, never quite got used to the high life and constant pressures of celebrity status, and finally turned to alcohol as a form of escapism. He is famously remembered for his humerous quotation,

I spent a lot of money on booze, birds and fast cars – the rest I just squandered.

On the Wagon

Best's drunken behaviour was at times untenable and on one occasion he stole from a lady's handbag on a beach to fund his alcohol addiction. He was arrested twice for drunken driving and swore profusely on national TV. During the course of his enforced rehabilitation, he was prescribed an Anti-Alcohol drug called Antabuse (disulfiram). This medication was first prescribed in the 1950s and right up until the 1990s was the only drug used in this way to help people stop drinking. Its efficacy is owing to its effect of making an alcoholic feel sick upon ingestion of a drink. In fact, the reaction to a solitary drink has been compared by some to suffering from food poisoning. This highly unpleasant effect in turn reduces the desire to drink alcohol allowing for recovery. Not everyone is suited to Antabuse though, i.e. those with heart, kidney or liver disease, those who are pregnant or are trying to be, or those who suffer from severe depression. George Best's career was ruined owing to his drinking habit and he suffered severe liver damage and subsequently pneumonia as a result. He received a highly controversial National Health Service liver transplant but sadly, the damage was already done. His sad but memorable final message to the world, one particularly aimed at other alcoholics was,

Don't die like me!

By learning to associate a negative outcome (feelings of nausea) with the previously highly desired experience (the taste of alcohol), the drinker is soon dissuaded from enjoying alcohol any longer, so eventually even the smell of alcohol is abhorrent to him. Research has shown that this method can have long-term success in maintaining abstinence (Wiens and Menustik, 1983).

There are more modern advances in the understanding of the brain processes which trigger and maintain addiction. A new class of **medication** has been developed, known as opiate antagonists, which play around with the neurotransmitters in our brain. Thus, the expected and pleasurable effects previously anticipated by the alcoholic are non-forthcoming and eliminated by the use of these drugs. Research is being carried out into medications such as naltrexone and nalmefene acamprosate, which might reduce the risk of relapse and subsequent return to drink. These drugs show great promise, particularly when used alongside anti-depressants, encouraging the individual to think more positively about a life without alcohol.

Psychoanalysis, a method traditionally concerned with verbal techniques of therapy: talking about traumatic childhood memories, free association and bringing a person's unconscious state to their consciousness, has advanced significantly since the days when an addict was told to lie back on a couch and pour out their hearts (imparting all their, as yet, unrevealed desires) and empty their pockets (to pay the analyst's extortionate fees). Owing to this unfortunate reputation, many people reject this option and still harbour a mistrust for the practice. In reality, evidence shows that psychoanalysis has many benefits for the recovering alcoholic and is nowadays being used much more frequently.

This form of therapy acknowledges that it is not the alcohol *per se* which makes an addict feel the compulsion to drink but is rather down to the individual himself, their unique personality make up and repressed memories of past experiences. Alcohol is used as a protective barrier for a lot of people, for example to help them relax, to forget, to cope and to go into denial of unwelcome or dreaded life events. The focus of this particular therapy is on the person's specific set of circumstances – their personal history, their needs, hopes and fears etc., all factors which are drawn out from the subconscious and dealt with individually, through discussion with the therapist. Long gone are the days when the client did all the talking, now the therapist also bears in mind the alcoholic's reluctance and sometimes terror in actually doing something positive to give up their addiction and will help him face his fears and advise him accordingly. True motivations are revealed during these sessions and, by taking responsibility for his own actions, the client has empowerment placed back in his hands to progress with overcoming *all* his problems, not just the alcohol dependency.

A modern treatment beneficial for recovering alcoholics is **Motivational Enhancement Therapy**. Therapist and patient work together to design a plan for recovery and to explore the benefits for that particular individual to refrain from drinking. It is also one of the most cost-effective methods available at present. This is classified as a self-help method and the patient will be given a set of stages (often twelve steps) to work towards to achieve full recovery. By dividing the course of recovery into manageable parts like this, the patient always has something to work towards and will feel pride in their determination and ability to maintain abstinence.

This recommendation is not going to meet with instant approval because of the stigma of the profession, but **psychiatrists** specialise in the workings of the mind and have serious qualifications and experience to deal with the addiction, the brain malfunction, which after all is what you have got. You can call him a 'shrink' (or any other name you like) but his job is to help people like you to get their lives back in order and start enjoying it again without the magnetism of alcohol to ruin things for you. Your local GP should know of one in your area and maybe even be able to organise an appointment for you at minimal or no cost to yourself, depending on your circumstances.

Some alcoholics advocate the use of acupuncture as part of their recovery programme. Your doctor is able to get your name on the waiting list for this sort of treatment, usually carried out by trained physiotherapists at your local hospital. Acupuncture is used for a multitude of different purposes from arthritis and tennis elbow to phobias and constant cravings of any sort too. With alcoholism being of the latter category,

On the Wagon

acupuncture is often said to reduce the urge to drink whilst increasing energy levels at the same time. It provides the recovering alcoholic with a different type of safeguard against PAWS (Post Acute Withdrawal syndrome). Not everyone finds it works for them to the same degree but it is an option worth considering, as so many swear by it for their individual problem.

Having researched various contemporary strategies to overcome addiction, one of the most effective seems to be in the use of a combination of therapeutic methods. Problem-solving approaches involve group sessions such as AA, a professional therapist and crisis intervention, ensuring the individual has the benefits of all – self-help co-operation, peer support and specialist knowledge and training of the therapist.

Any sexual dysfunction issues are normally resolved upon abstinence. At first the changes in your body and even the way you think will be alien to you but are all good signs of recovery. You may find you begin to have increased libido, more stamina and generally enjoy and make your partner enjoy sex more. If problems still occur after giving up the drink for some time, see a doctor. Erectile dysfunction can be caused by other underlying conditions such as diabetes and there is normally more than one contributory factor. Alcohol alone cannot be entirely blamed and this needs to be checked out. The doctor may prescribe a drug to help with erectile disorder such as Viagra. There are also gimmicky products on the market, like the penis pump to increase blood flow and to help sustain erection for longer. Work stress is a common factor but problems can be exacerbated if the partner then misconstrues the apparent loss of performance as a sign of rejection, their own failings or even of infidelity. Religious, ethnic and cultural differences can also inhibit couples from talking about their problem with each other. A **sexual therapist** can help by identifying the conditions which contribute to the problem and then a relevant set of techniques, tailor-made to the couple in question, can be taught to overcome these. Anxiety reduction is one such technique. Information is also provided about the complex sexual reproductive system so that couples are more aware of what goes on during intercourse. Medical checks are also given to rule out additional physiological problems.

If you are feeling that you can no longer cope with your situation but would like to discuss the matter with someone in total confidence, there are special hotlines designed to provide the caller with round-the-clock advice and support. These **Crisis Intervention** centres have psychiatrists, psychologists and social workers at your disposal, in addition to non-professional volunteers, trained to help people in their time of need. Not only intended to be there for people with a drinking problem, they also deal with traumas such as domestic violence, rape and flood victims. They can offer the best advice given the circumstances but are also ready to act and get

On the Wagon

someone to the caller quickly if they feel they are in danger from self-harming or having suicidal thoughts.

In order to decide upon the appropriate course of action to help an individual with his or her addiction, the professional will first need to carry out a **preliminary screening** to assess the client's degree of dependence. He will already have received a basic report from the GP or other person requesting intervention but to have the greatest chance of success and to prevent relapse the professional will need to establish some important data to help him draw his conclusions. It is important to note here the difference between a screening and an assessment. The screening is intended to primarily identify those with a severe alcohol-related problem or who are at risk of developing one, whereas the more in depth assessment is carried out to obtain more detailed information about the drinker in order to form an in-depth diagnosis and to decide upon the appropriate treatment.

During the course of the initial **assessment**, an opinion will be formed as to whether the alcoholic has the necessary coping skills, the support of other familial members and the propensity for change, all necessary in the treatment of the client's addiction. He will also need to be convinced that the person needing help is fully aware of the positive benefits of abstaining and equally, the negative consequences of not doing so. A failure to acknowledge the elementary benefits of giving up alcohol, smoking, drugs, inhalants or gambling-related disorders costs governments and national health systems millions and, in addition to the well-being of the individual, there are other major factors to be considered before substantial costs are invested into the treatment of someone who has no intention at all to change their anti-social behaviour. As the estimated economic costs in the USA reached $223.5 in 2006 alone, it is not a decision to be taken lightly to put this client forward for treatment unless one can be certain of a small amount of commitment and determination at least. A shocking 88,000 people die each year in America as a direct result of alcoholism. Loss of workplace productivity accounts for a huge 72% of these national expenses, 11% is spent on health care, 9% on criminal justice and law enforcement and 6% on vehicle crashes caused by those drinking and causing motor vehicle crashes (source CDC – Centers for Disease Control and Prevention).

The following section will serve to act as an insight into some of the assessment techniques used by professionals, so that alcoholics and those who wish to help them, have at least some inkling as to the sort of questions which will be asked, although for the purpose of this book, these diagnostic instruments are inevitably far from exhaustive.

Referral to a professional will include several measures, designed to establish the severity of alcohol dependence and whether the individual and those who live with the alcoholic are at risk in any way. He will also be equipped to make some speculation as to the likely consequences of alcohol withdrawal for the person in question.

There are numerous alcohol screening tests available to professionals, often referred to by an acronym formed from key words or assessment measures used. For example, the CAGE (Ewing, 1984), entails four questions being asked of the alcoholic:

1. "Have you ever felt the need to *Cut* down on your drinking?"
2. "Have you ever felt *Annoyed* by someone criticizing your drinking?"
3. "Have you ever felt bad or *Guilty* about your drinking?"
4. "Have you ever had a drink first thing in the morning to steady your nerves and get rid of a hangover [*Eye-opener*]?"

Although this is a very quick test to administer (between one and two minutes), the responses rely on the person's memory and complete honesty. As the questions are all in the past tense, they might not glean knowledge as to a current problem or give an accurate bearing on alcohol consumption. It is however a good first screening to detect dependence and can be carried out by virtually anyone, professional or not. Any on-the-spur-of-the-moment questioning like this has the potential to reveal more of the true situation than some long and drawn out tests administered by computer responses and only needs to highlight *two* possible responses before alcohol dependence is identified.

The addition of an extra question, "When was the last time you had more than four drinks (for females) and five (for men) in one day?", if responded to with a date within the last three months, has been found to accurately detect individuals with current drinking disorders and allows the professional to make reasonable assumptions as to the degree of withdrawal symptoms which will be experienced on abstinence.

Each time a new screening measure is devised, it purports to be better in some way than those preceding it. The RAPS, a 5-item test was created, based on the success of several other tests but with minor tweaks to outperform the others, until a 93% accurate diagnosis of alcohol dependency could be given, consistently appropriate across genders and ethnic minority groups (Cherpitel, 1995).

1. "During the last year, have you had a feeling of guilt or remorse after drinking?" (Remorse).
2. "During the last year, has a friend or family member ever told you about things you said or did while you were drinking that you could not remember?" (Amnesia)
3. "During the last year, have you failed to do what was normally expected of you because of drinking?" (Performance)

4. "Do you sometimes take a drink in the morning when you first get up?" (Starter).

Sometimes, elaboration on the responses, can assist the professional in forming a judgement as to the alcoholic's true desire to change their compulsion to drink and to their level of motivation to stop. Confirming feelings of guilt is all well and good but does not necessarily guarantee a determination to cut back or abstain, although they can send the drinker into a deeper state of helplessness and depression.

The most commonly used source for diagnostic assessment in clinical settings in the USA is the DSM (now on its fifth edition, as of 2013). In England and other countries, reference is made to the ICD-10 (International Classification of Diseases), published by the WHO (World Health Organisation, 1992), although both resources rely on similar criteria in the diagnosis of alcohol-related problems.

Given the high degree of comorbidity between alcoholism and other mental disorders, the above sources are an effective means for the professional of identifying one problem from another. To the 'moderate' drinker, it might not be obvious why someone who is wholly dependent on alcohol cannot simply cut down on his consumption a little and yet still enjoy a twice weekly drink for example. Research studies have shown however that those displaying a greater dependence severity are less likely to be ideal candidates for moderate drinking outcomes (Rosenberg, 1993), so these people are better suited to total abstinence.

Once undeniable alcohol dependence has been confirmed, and the degree of its severity, a reasonably accurate measure of alcohol consumption has to be determined. As responses to assessment questions are usually based on self-report, it is important to interview the person under suitable conditions. To enhance the validity of these assessments, it is logical to ensure the individual has not consumed any alcohol prior to the assessment, that strict confidence is assured, that the interview is carried out in a setting which does not punish admissions of drinking and that it is determined without doubt, the type, alcohol content and normal serving size of the respondent's preferred alcohol drink. Quantity-Frequency (QF) measures are then applied, using diary notes made regarding heavy versus lighter drinking days, and whether heavier drinking days are regular or sporadic. Retrospective estimations of drinking are undeniably problematic and the use of daily drinking diaries is therefore highly recommended. No method of assessment is infallible and all rely on the respondent's honesty and accurate self-monitoring. Faked compliance, whereby missed entries are completed at a time in the future, also tends to confuse the issue. Modern technology now relies on an Interactive Voice Response (IVR), in which participants phone a computer-automated interviewing system to record their drinking habits on a daily basis. The benefit of this method is in its confidentiality and lack of interviewer effects.

On the Wagon

Of course the most reliable assessment of alcohol consumption is a biological one. Carried out in conjunction with self-reports, this has a high degree of efficacy and reliability. Alcohol biomarkers can be detected by the measurement of *ethanol,* the addictive ingredient of alcohol, in the body. This substance can be found in a person's breath, serum, urine or saliva. In clinical or law enforcement settings, there are virtually no false positive results, the only drawback being the speed at which ethanol disappears from the blood. This test is therefore only reliable for alcohol consumption within the last 6-8 hours and may even give a false negative reading if the drinker has abstained on the actual day of the test.

If a person is a regular and heavy consumer of alcohol, a much more reliable test is the Serum *gamma-glutamyl transpeptidase* (GGT), which measures functionality of the liver, the main organ to be affected by excessive alcohol consumption. These tests are relatively inexpensive and widely available but readings can be elevated by certain disorders including diabetes, hypertension and obesity.

We can therefore now see that much time, co-operation and money has to be invested into the cause of helping someone refrain from their drinking addiction. It is never as easy as being able to drink one day and then give up the next. The body will have been affected and abused in many ways by excessive alcohol consumption but will also, ironically be temporarily affected by sudden abstinence.

In Chapter 3, we discussed the unpleasant side effects which may be experienced on abstinence from alcohol, one of the worst of which was Delirium Tremors or DTs. The good news is that all those side effects cease if a week elapses without alcohol. This is then a particularly vulnerable time for those wishing to go 'on the wagon' and therefore, those trying to help an alcoholic give up drinking must deny all access to alcohol during this crucial time. From having spoken to people who have undergone treatment for alcoholism, it would seem that:

- Following abstinence, withdrawal symptoms such as shaking hands and palpitations will cease after about a week has elapsed.

- A professional treatment programme will last for about a month but will then require some aftercare in the form of follow-up meetings to discuss progress, to offer motivation and support.

- The most effective programmes seem to include a mixture of care: individual therapy (one-to-one with a professional), therapy as part of a group or with members of your family and any necessary medical treatment to help physical recovery.

On the Wagon

- The first six months are the hardest, when relapse, the slipping back into the addictive behaviour, is most likely to occur. Many alcoholics have been known to relapse at some point or other, so aftercare is crucial for a successful recovery. This is a major milestone however, and having reached this length of time without alcohol, chances of continued success substantially increase.

It is not realistic to assume that every alcoholic presenting for treatment is equally motivated to follow through with the substantial changes necessary to achieve long-term sobriety. This readiness to give up something that has been depended on for so long will not be available with the flick of a switch. Society's social acceptance of drinking, as opposed to drug taking is like a carrot dangling in front of the proverbial ass, added to the simplicity of access to this particular substance. The ability to resist a drink varies considerably between individuals, with those who easily give in to temptation being most at risk. Coping skills are often a very important part of any rehabilitation treatment. These skills are particularly helpful in managing and preparing for potential relapse situations. Some studies suggest that a person's spirituality and religiosity can offer additional help in the fight against relapse (Miller, Westerberg, Harris & Tonigan, 1996). Role play is used to help the addict predict their own response to different drinking scenarios when he may need to decline a drink whilst under social pressure to do otherwise. Self-esteem and taking pride in these autonomous decisions are also two factors which will give the alcoholic strength to continue in his resolve.

Having a **good social network** of friends and family members is also essential. Being able to talk to others who have undergone similar treatment is beneficial as is any sort of support to maintain the determination to give up drinking.

Watching some **motivational films** is a good idea as you can compare your situation to the actors' and empathise with their personal traumas. You then get to see how they manage to free themselves of their addiction and build new lives. The films might inspire you in your quest for sobriety and even encourage you to volunteer to help others overcome their drinking problems in the future. Here are just a few:

28 Days
This film stars Sandra Bullock and depicts a woman with a successful career, who drinks too much and consequently crashes her car. She also ruins her own sister's wedding. At first she declines any help and is in denial of her problem. However she is made to receive rehabilitation and initially goes against that too. Eventually she is forced to acknowledge the problem she has and decides to take positive action to restart her life without alcohol. The film demonstrates how alcoholics can achieve this

On the Wagon

when they are able to see the trouble they are causing, both for themselves and others as well.

My Name is Bill W
A 1989 film based on the true life story of Bill Wilson, one of the original founders of Alcoholics Anonymous. Bill was a successful businessman who floundered and became an alcoholic. The story tells of his several attempts to become sober but eventually he finds a method which works for him. When he forms a relationship with another alcoholic, the two men form a group to help others in the same quest which forms the basis for the founding of AA, the successful support group, well known across the world today.

The Basketball Diaries
Another true story which depicts a young man who had a promising career as a basketball player but who then turned to heroin. Despite the fact that this film does not have alcohol as its main theme, it shows how a dependency can make someone lose their self-respect and cause them much difficulty getting back on the straight and narrow. Released in 1995, Leonardo DiCaprio is the main character who resorts to selling his body to pay for his habit. The film is eventful with the protagonist spending a stretch in prison and then in a mental institution. There is however a happy ending with the addict pulling through and getting his life back together.

Drunks
A 1995 film, revolving around an AA meeting. This is a poignant film showing how alcohol not only destroys lives but also shows how some individuals can manage to escape their addiction. Both simple and credible this film helps those in recovery remain aware of their goal and how their lives will improve when they give up drinking.

Days of Wine and Roses
A much older film (1962) but one which is still good. Jack Lemmon plays an alcoholic named Joe Clay and demonstrates how addiction can have a detrimental effect on relationships. When he meets a woman he coerces her into drinking with him but their escapades soon have a dreadful impact on their lives resulting in a distressing event. The principal character is admitted to a psychiatric ward and begins rebuilding his life with the help of AA, whilst his drinking partner refuses to seek help and therefore does not have such a fortunate outcome.

Clean and Sober
Michael Keaton is both a cocaine user and alcoholic in this film. His career as a real estate agent goes downhill and his drinking habits cause him to suffer from amnesia. When he wakes, he does not recognise the woman in his bed but worse still she appears to have overdosed. He is then erroneously blamed for money going

missing at work and decides to enter rehab, purely to evade his problems. Eventually his resolve to become clean and sober increases and he is able to overcome his addictions.

When a Man Loves a Woman

This 1994 film stars Meg Ryan and Andy Garcia, a married couple who appear to have just about everything. Owing to his profession however, the husband is away much of the time and fails to notice the warning signs that his wife is an alcoholic. It is only when she reneges on her responsibilities that it becomes evident that she needs help to become sober. Ironically, the husband then finds it hard to reconcile that he now has a wife who is different to before, one who is independent and no longer reliant on alcohol.

The Lost Weekend

A very old film but one which made its mark back in 1945 and which is still highly relevant now. It contains a powerful message about addiction and focuses on the life of an alcoholic and events which occur whilst he is on a bender. Flashbacks come to him as a constant reminder of how his life was destroyed by alcohol and how he lost everything of value to him as a result of his drinking. Towards the end of the film there is an emotional speech which should be heeded by us all about the effects of alcoholism.

Not all these films will be to your taste (or mine either) but they may help you to acknowledge your problem and come as a warning to the consequences of excess drinking. They should also impart some insight as to how to overcome the addiction and how to move on, as a person with clear judgement and unclouded foresight into how a life should be without a dependency.

The transition from severe alcoholic to teetotaler is far from being an easy one. Nobody will try to convince you otherwise. In fact no one can promise that you won't pick up a glass of alcohol again. The temptations in life are far too many and complex to offer us any amount of certainty but the difference giving up will make to your life is immeasurable and well worth the effort. If you remain a heavy drinker, you could lose your job, your partner and your home. You could lose every single thing you value in life and if the drinking gets out of hand, lives could be lost too. Just for the sake of another glass of alcohol, it is not worth all the distress caused. Live each day as it comes and do something positive with your life. Make the decision to 'go on the wagon', get the necessary support and stick to your resolve. Do not hold it against anyone who wishes to help see you through this situation and who seeks help on your behalf. Early intervention is vital to minimise complications and I am sure you will thank them later. It will change your life for good and you will be a much happier, healthier and successful person for making that change. Recently I have personally watched two

On the Wagon

people make that monumental change and they have not touched one single drink since. These people were on the verge of self-destruction - one lost his wife and access to his children as a result of his drinking, while the other whittled away his money and lost the respect of his family and friends. If these two can do it, believe me, you can definitely succeed too.

References

Brown, G. L., Goodwin, F. K., Ballenger, J. C., Goyer, P.F.et al., (1979). Aggression in humans correlates with cerebrospinal fluid amine metabolites, *Psychiatry Research, 1,* 131-139.

Cherpitel, C. J. (1995). Screening for alcohol problems in the emergency room: A rapid alcohol problems screen. *Drug and Alcohol Dependence, 40,* 133-137.

Chick, J., Aschauer, H., Hornik, K., and Group, I. (2004). Efficacy of fluvoxamine in preventing relapse in alcohol dependence: A one-year, double-blind, placebo-controlled multicenter study with analysis by typology. – *Drug and Alcohol Dependence, 74* (1), 61-70.

Darley, J. M., Glucksberg, S., Kamin, L. J. and Kinchla, R. A. (1984). *Psychology,* Second Edition, New Jersey: Prentice-Hall, Inc.

Ewing, J. (1984). Detecting alcoholism: The CAGE questions. *Journal of the American Medical Association, 252,* 1905-1907.

Higley, J.D., Mehlman, P.T., Taub, D. M., Higley, S. B. et al., (1992). Cerebrospinal fluid monoamine and adrenal correlates of aggression in free-ranging rhesus monkeys, *Archives of General Psychiatry, 49,* 436-441.

Hucker, C.O. (1975). *China's Imperial Past,* Stanford, CA: Stanford University Press.

Kruesi, M. J. (1979). Cruelty to animals and CSF 5HIAA, *Psychiatry Research, 28,* 115-116.

Lutz, H.F. (1922). *Viticulture and Brewing in the Ancient Orient,* New York: J.C. Heinrichs.

Miller, W.R., Westerberg, V.S., Harris, R.J. & Tonigan,J.S. (1996). What predicts relapse?: Prospective testing of antecedent models. *Addiction, 91* (Suppl.), S155-S171.

National Institute on Alcohol Abuse and Alcoholism (1995). *The physician's guide to helping patients with alcohol problems* (NIH Publication No. 95-3769). United States Public Health Service.

National Institute on Alcohol Abuse and Alcoholism (N.I.A.A.A., 2000) http://www.niaaa.com.

Patrick, C H. (1952). *Alcohol, Culture, and Society*, NC: Duke University Press, Durham, Reprint edition by AMS Press, New York, 1970.

Rockville, M.D. (2000). U.S. Department of Health and Human Services, *10th Special Report to Congress on Alcohol and Health.*

Rosenberg, H. (1993). Prediction of controlled drinking by alcoholics and problem drinkers. *Psychological Bulletin, 113,* 129-139.

Substance Abuse and Mental Health Services Administration, Office of Applied Studies. Results from the 2007 National Survey on Drug Use and Health: National Findings. Rockville, MD: 2008. (NSDUH Series H-34, DHHS Publication No. SMA 08-4343).

Wiens, A. N. and Menustik, C. E. (1983). Treatment outcome and patient characteristics in an aversion therapy program for alcoholism. *American Psychologist,* 38, 1089-96.

World Health Organization, (1992). *The ICD-10 classification of mental and behavioural disorders: Clinical descriptions and diagnostic guidelines.*

Lightning Source UK Ltd.
Milton Keynes UK
UKHW02f1845130618
324207UK00028B/544/P